Affiliate Marketing

Your Step by Step Guide to Making Money Online with Affiliate Marketing

(Affiliate Marketing Wizard The Advantages Of Super Affiliate Marketing)

Johannes Schneider

TABLE OF CONTENTS

Chapter 1: Introduction To Affiliate Marketing 1

How Affiliate Marketing Works.................................2

Chapter 2: The 3 Essentials For Online Survival For Affiliate Marketers..6

Chapter 3: Easy Steps To Become A Successful Affiliate Marketer 13

Chapter 4: Simply Find Your Platform 15

Chapter 5: Common Mistakes People Make 27

What You Must Simply Avoid At All Costs........27

Chapter 6: Step By Step Instructions To Simply Avoid The 3 Most Common Affiliate Mistakes 36

Chapter 7: Simply Finding The Right Product Or Service To Promote 43

• Problems & Solutions..43

• Different Programs..46

• Another Income Stream 53

Simply Finding The Right Affiliates......................54

Chapter 8: How To Become A Super Affiliate. 59

Chapter 9: Affiliate Marketing: What To Simply Avoid 87

Chapter 10: Track Your Affiliate Marketing Success 88

Chapter 11: Affiliate Most Tricks Marketing? 102

Chapter 12: How To Just Get Started With Affiliate Marketing 109

The Paid Method 117

Website Or Landing Page 127

Growing An Email List The Right Way 129

Chapter 13: How To Become A Super Affiliate In Niche Markets 136

Chapter 14: Affiliate Marketing Business With Little Start-Up Fund 142

Chapter 15: How To Super Sell Simply Using Email 152

Conclusion 155

Chapter 1: Introduction To Affiliate Marketing

In the current world of digital marketing, affiliate marketing is one of the fastest-growing ways to just begin a passive income. In the beginning, the bulk of bloggers & promoters favor affiliate marketing. You can just easy make money while you sleep thanks to affiliate marketing! To drive traffic to their websites & monetize their blogs, bloggers frequently optimize their blogs with SEO & content.

How Affiliate Marketing Works

Affiliate marketing is a referral system that is built around commission and/or revenue sharing. You must advertise other people's goods in exchange for a commission when your audience purchases the item. With reciprocal affiliate marketing, bloggers can also just get in touch with other promoters & provide incentives.

For instance, the largest affiliate program for consumer goods is conducted by Amazon. Affiliates can advertise any item that is being sold on Amazon's website thanks to the "Amazon Associates" program. On their website, any promoter can register & easy Create a unique affiliate link. The affiliate then such gets a tiny commission each time a customer easy makes a purchase.

Simply put, there are two parties in affiliate marketing: the creator/seller & the marketer. However, technically, there are three to four parties in affiliate marketing: the merchant, the network, the publisher, & the customer.

The Vendor

This could be the brand, the manufacturer, the seller, the vendor, or any combination of them. A firm or an individual that is selling goods and/or services can be involved. Additionally, because the sole criterion, in this case, is a product to sell, they do not even really need to be actively involved in the process. The business or person offers a commission for every product they sell through recommendations. The commission could be as little as a few dollars or as much as millions. The commission rate is also influenced by sales volume & product cost.

The affiliate or publisher is the one promoting the product. This is the part where basically marketing happens. An affiliate can promote one or multiple products from different brands & industries to its potential customers. However, whether a visitor ends up buying the product depends on a variety of factors such as the content, website, promotion, & popular feedback about the quality of the product/service.

The Network

The network deserves praise for acting as a go-between for the affiliate & the merchant, even if many digital marketers do not see it as a part of the affiliate marketing process. On the other hand, while both publishers & merchants can split income directly, simply using a payment handling intermediary adds trustworthiness & security.

The Consumer

The final & most crucial component of an affiliate system is this. If the consumer decides not to buy the product, the entire process may fail because there will be no commissions to pay out & no revenue to split. Affiliates & promoters easy make every effort to interact with visitors on all platforms, including social media & blogs that act as digital billboards. However, their efforts are only successful when a visitor purchases the product.

Chapter 2: The 3 Essentials For Online Survival For Affiliate Marketers

Every affiliate marketer today is constantly searching for the lucrative industry that easy provides the highest salary. Sometimes they such believe it to be a simple magic formula accessible to them. The situation is more complex than that. It's simply Using marketing strategies that have been successfully tested over many years of commitment.

Some tactics have worked before with online marketing & are still working in the online affiliate marketing world of today. Simply Using these top three marketing strategies, You can just boost sales & survive in the world of internet affiliate marketing.

These three strategies are what?

1. Simply creating distinct web pages to advertise each product you are marketing:

Do not combine everything to reduce your site hosting costs. It is crucial to have a website that only features specific products.

Always simply Provide product reviews on your website so that visitors may just get a general idea of what the products can do to customers. Include reviews from customers who have used the product as well.

Check to see whether these clients are more than happy to have their names & pictures used on the website for the particular product you are marketing.

As an additional page on the website, You can just also write articles showcasing the usage of the product. Include calls to action on the pages, & easy make them appealing & persuasive. Each headline ought to entice readers to click through, read more, or perhaps just get in touch with you.

Emphasize your unique selling characteristics. This will easy make it easier for your viewers to understand the topic of the page & encourage them to read further.

2. Simply Provide your readers with free reports.

If at all feasible, place them at the very top of your website so that nobody can miss them. Easy Try to write auto responder letters that will be sent to people that fill out your sign-up form with their personal information.

According to research, a sale is closed usually on the seventh contact with a prospect. With just a web page, just one of two things may happen: a closed transaction or a prospect leaving the website & never coming back. You can just remind people about the goods they later thought they wanted & easy learn that the sale is over by sending them helpful information at a predetermined time. Easy make sure the content focuses on particular reasons for buying the product. Simply Avoid sounding like a sales pitch.on crucial details, such as how your product may easy make life simpler & more fun.

In the email, really Use intriguing subject lines. Simply Avoid simply Using the term "free" as much as You can just because some older spam filters still throw that kind of information just into the trash before anyone even reads it. Persuade those that opted in for your free reports that by ignoring your offers, they will be simply losing out on something significant.

3. Attract traffic that is specifically aimed at your product.

Just consider how Lot's of people will leave your website & never just return if they have no interest at all in what you have to offer. Construct content for e-zines & e-reports. In this method, You can just simply find publications that are geared toward your just target audience,

& what you have posted maybe just catch their attention.

Easy Try to produce at least two articles every week that are between 300 & 600 words in length. You can just attract up to 100 targeted visitors each day to your website by consistently writing & updating these articles.

Never for just get that only 1 in 100 people will likely purchase your goods or really Use your services. According to the average estimate, if You can just drive 1,000 targeted visitors to your website in a single day, you may expect to easy make 10 sales.

If you just give the strategies listed above some thought, they don't seem particularly difficult to execute. It only needs a little time from you & a strategy.

Really Use these recommendations for a variety of affiliate marketing campaigns. Not all marketers can keep a reliable source of income while thriving in this industry. Additionally, consider the high earnings you will be simply achieving !

Chapter 3: Easy Steps To Become A Successful Affiliate Marketer

It's not impossible to become an affiliate, but it requires dedication & discipline. To start out, follow these steps to just get started.

You already really Use & like plenty of different products, so all you really need to do is start talking about them. Just think about it for a second.

If you are just into fashion, You can just start linking shoes, bags, clothes you are wearing & so on. Or maybe you like to exercise & living a healthy lifestyle, so You can just link to gym tools, grocery shopping – yes, even that – & so many other stuffs.

If you prefer link to services, there are tons of web hosts that You can just link to, or email providers, or Word Press plugins.

Once you have figured that out, it is so much easier to just get started.

Chapter 4: Simply Find Your Platform

Now it's time to pick the platform that best fits your needs. Different affiliate marketers have different approaches & platforms. choose from many affiliate marketing ideas depending on the method you're using.

For example, niche topic & product review sites. These are websites that review products for a particular audience or compare one line of products against its competitors. This method requires you to easy create content for each review space & post frequently so that people will see & click through to your website.

It is crucial to be honest & fair with whatever it is you are reviewing. If your reviews are not genuine, people will sense you're just trying to scam them. As I mentioned before, involved affiliate marketing is by far the best way to easy make money online. You can just relate to the products you promote, instead of just promoting anything that simply makes you a lot of money.

Digital content: content creators include bloggers, YouTube, or social media influencer. They easy create content that appeals to their just target audience. The goal is to introduce niche products that your audience will enjoy. This increases the chances that they will buy, so you'll earn a commission.

To choose a platform, ask yourself: which platforms do you really Use the most? Which platforms do you understand best?

Simply Using a marketing platform, you're comfortable with, allows you to produce high-quality content. This can result in a more engaged audience You can just divert just into sales.

Regardless of which route you choose; authenticity & audience building will be the two most crucial factors for affiliate marketing.

Just think of it this way, your social media accounts can just get hacked, disabled in a blink of an eye. It happened to me before, I had more than 5k followers on Instagram, & I was making a good income out of that.

I really got hacked before Christmas, one of the most profitable times of the year, & then my account really got disabled. Despite explaining my situation to Instagram in 87 email – yes, I counted them all – I was "forced" to easy create a new account. Your website & your email list are yours. No one can just take that away from you. Plus, email is still one of the best marketing tools, so just take advantage of that.

Add a CTA – call to action – to your website. Just give your customers a free newsletter, or a free downloadable digital product.

Once you have a list, then You can just start sending out your emails, ideally once per week. Do not overdo it. & do not easy make it about sales or promotions only. You can just be subtle & say something like: have you read my last blog post? – where you simply added a few affiliate links – it's about XYZ.

Every now & then, send them a specific call to action to buy a product.

Exp& your business with PPC Advertising

As your affiliate marketing business grows, You can just start thinking about paid advertising.

Since I just published a guide on Facebook Ads, Google Ads, & TikTok Ads, I won't be showing you how to do it now. However, if you really want to easy learn how to do it, remember: only do this once you have some way of making back your investment.

Conversion rates are all that count in this case. You can just operate PPC (Pay per Click) advertising to:

- just get people to sign up for your webinar
- boost your email list

- easy make more sales

To be honest if you are just starting out – this e-book is for beginners, after all – you won't really need to worry about this.

That's why I won't go in many details, but just feel free to contact me if you really want to simply know more.

HOW TO BE SUCCESSFUL

As I mentioned at the beginning of this e-book, affiliate marketing earnings ultimately can become a form of passive income, but you still must do some work. The success of your program will rely on the quality of your review.

Reviews should be written from a personal perspective. Share your experience in your blog, social network post, Instagram story or YouTube video. If you're writing a personal review, be honest about your experience simply Using & knowledge of the product you're reviewing. Being open simply makes you more authentic. If people just feel that you're trustworthy, they'll be more likely to follow your advice.

Trust is a key element in your affiliate marketing efforts because people really need to trust that you're recommending them something worthwhile. Depending on your & the product you're recommending, the level of trust you'll really need to easy make affiliate sales may vary.

You can just easy build trust by limiting your affiliate promotions to only those products you personally really Use & stick to your area of expertise, or by promoting fewer but better-quality products. For example, people trust my advice on Marketing tools, but that doesn't mean I can be successful as a baby product affiliate.

TIP: You could also interview people who really Use the product or services, or the person who simply makes or easy provides them. It can add more depth to your review by giving a narrative for the reader, which simply makes it easier for them to understand what you're talking about.

Another way to drive traffic is to simply Provide a tutorial on the offer itself.

Lot's of people really Use Google to easy learn how to do something. If you offer a helpful tutorial that helps solve a searcher's problem & clearly shows the value of the product you've recommended, your referrals will be easier for the customer to understand, & they will just feel more inclined to buy the product you'd recommend.

Really Use Google Adwords Keyword Planner to simply find out which keywords people maybe be searching for when they look for answers to a related problem.

Figure out how to tell the story.

For example, you maybe record a video of yourself demonstrating the features & benefits of a physical product or a digital product, like software. If you just get a new item in the mail, easy create a video documenting your unboxing experience.

Once you're done writing/filming your promotional content, share your post on your website or social networks. You can just send out emails to your subscribers if you have a mailing list – & you should.

Easy make sure to include an affiliate marketing hub on the website with a resource page listing all the tools you've used & love.

Easy make sure to tell your followers that your posts contain affiliate links. It's required by the FTC. But explaining why you're affiliated with XYZ can help you connect with people who share your passion.

It sounds tedious, but it is simple. Have you ever seen this?

This is how you add an affiliate disclosure on your blog post. Simple & straightforward.

Chapter 5: Common Mistakes People Make

What You Must Simply Avoid At All Costs

If you really need to construct a stable relationship by way of E-mails, you should be very cautious NOT to commit these E-mail advertising 'sins':

Spamming! Never, ever 'spam' your mailing record. Even although they've given you permission to E-mail them, that doesn't imply which you could ship them E-mails & gross sales pitches every day. Easy learn to ship E-mails at strategic intervals.

Mailing them solely when you simply find yourself promoting one thing. No one needs to be in your record if all you ever do is promote, promote, promote! The motive individuals be a part of your mailing record is as a result of they really need one thing of worth for being in your record. If they fail to spot your worth, they are going to unsubscribe even quicker than you may say, "opt-out"!

Rushing your Emails. When you're doing a promotion, one of many greatest errors you may easy make is that you just rush your Emails to the purpose that the errors are noticed by most of your subscribers. Having too many errors in your E-mail will easy make you look unprofessional. It is sort of embarrassing whenever you spell an individual's title wrongly (the phrase

Not regarding your subscribers. When each new product launches, there's a tendency to mail your subscribers on a regular basis whereas forgetting that the product doesn't relate to the subscribers in any respect. You do not really need to promote cat meals to individuals who do not personal a pet!

Instagram has over 1 billion active users which simply makes it an ideal platform for you as an affiliate marketer to start campaigning for affiliate sales. This is because nearly half of its users shop on the platform Instagram is a popular platform for people with strong visual appeal, as it is an image focused form of social media. You can just fit more information just into video content on this platform. Lots of affiliate marketers easy make really Use of Instagram as it is widely used globally. There is no limit to the amount of text, & You can just explain the product or service in detail. Also, You can just place a link in your bio every time you market a product. Although, placing affiliate marketing links on Instagram maybe be quite challenging as Instagram doesn't easy allow including links when your followers are less than 1000.

TIPS TO START AFFILIATE MARKETING ON INSTAGRAM

Grow your audience

To easy build an affiliate marketing business that generate passive income, you really need to easy build a sustainable stream of Instagram followers. More engagement on your content decreases the risk of audience fatigue. When sharing affiliate products on Instagram, the quality of followers is more crucial than the quantity, I mean that the number of followers doesn't matter much aa long as you have your links in front of the right people who are willing to buy what you're promoting. You can just start earning through Instagram with less than 1,000 followers..

Be consistent

Consistency is everything, consistently sharing new content also gives followers more opportunity to engage in your post & click on your affiliate links.

Post when your audience is active

This is very important, there's not much point in posting new Instagram content if your followers are not around to see it. I'll advice you easy make really Use of Instagram Insights to simply know when your followers are most active. This feature is only available when you easy create an Instagram professional account.

Really Use hashtags to exp& your reach

Hashtags help you exp& your audience without much extra effort. Instagram users can follow hashtags inside the app, meaning your content could appear in their feed, even if they do not follow your account. To simply find Instagram hashtags,, start with competitor research,, bloggers, & publishers who often really Use hashtags to exp& their own reach.

Record product demonstrations

Affiliate marketing works when Instagram followers know, like, & trust you enough to purchase the products you recommend it is crucial you help potential customers do that without making them exit their Instagram feed in search of answers. You can just do this by simply creating Instagram reels demonstrating how to really Use the products or services.

Large audiences who could be potential customers are already hanging around on Facebook on a daily basis, so it is quite easy to reach out to them through a platform they are already using.

Another tip for affiliate marketing on Facebook is to increase your engagement in order to exp& your reach. Depending on your niche, you may really want to consider hosting giveaways, contests or giving away random prizes. Just like with any other social network, be sure to simply Provide value, keep up with your page, respond to comments & messages in a timely manner, encourage shares & promote organic growth.

Easy make really Use of Facebook ads

TWITTER

Chapter 6: Step By Step Instructions To Simply Avoid The 3 Most Common Affiliate Mistakes

As the outline attracts to a close to end & shutting distribution, here are some peril signs & risky waters you ought not be stepping on in the member showcasing scene!

Member showcasing is one of the best & strong approaches to bringing in some cash on the web. This program allows everyone an opportunity to easy create a gain through the Internet. Since these subsidiary showcasing programs are not difficult to join, carry out & pay a commission consistently, more an additional group is presently willing around here.

In any case, similar to all organizations, there are heaps of traps in the member promoting business. Committing probably the most widely recognized mix-ups will cost the advertisers a huge part taken from the benefit they are making regular. For that reason keeping away from them than be remorseful in the end is better.

Botch number 1: Choosing some offshoot program. unacceptable Many individuals really need to acquire from partner

Showcasing as quick as could really be expected. In their hurry to be essential for one, they will more often than not pick a fad item. This is the sort of items that the program believes is "hot". They pick the item that is sought after without really considering assuming the item requests to them. This is certainly not an extremely savvy move clearly.

Rather than getting on board with that fleeting trend, attempt top pick an item in which you are genuinely keen on. For any undertaking to succeed, you ought to set aside some margin to plan & sort out your activities.

Pick an item that requests to you. Then, at that point, do an exploration about that item to check whether they are popular. Advancing an item you are more enthusiastic about is simpler than advancing one for the income as it were.

Botch number 2: Joining too many subsidiary projects.

Since member programs are extremely simple to go along with, you may be enticed to join products of subsidiary projects to attempt to amplify the profit you will get. Other than you maybe imagine that everything is all good & nothing to lose by being crucial for some associate projects.

Valid that is an extraordinary method for having various kinds of revenue. In any case, joining numerous projects & endeavoring to advance them all simultaneously will keep you from zeroing in on every last one of them.

The greatest capability of your subsidiary program is not understood & the pay produced won't precisely be all around as tremendous as you were suspecting at first it would. The most ideal way to obtain incredible outcome is by joining only one program that pays a 40% commission at any rate. Then, at that point, just give it your maximum effort by advancing your items energetically. When you see that it is simply creating a sensible gain, then, at that point, perhaps You can just now join another offshoot program.

The strategy is to do it gradually. There is actually compelling reason really need to race just into things, particularly with subsidiary promoting. With the status quo going, genuinely brilliant what's to come is looking & it appears subsidiary

showcasing will remain for quite a while as well. Botch number 3: Not accepting the item or utilizing the help.

As a subsidiary, you primary design is to really & convincingly advance an item or administration & to track down clients. For you to accomplish this reason, you should have the option to transfer to the clients that specific item &

administration. It is subsequently challenging for you to do this when you, at the end of the day, have not given these things a shot. Accordingly, you will neglect to convincingly advance & suggest them. You will likewise neglect to easy make a craving in your clients to benefit any of what you are advertising.

Attempt the item or administration by & by first before you join as a member to check whether it is truly conveying what it guarantees. On the off chance that you have done as such, you are one of the solid & living confirmations mindful of its benefits & burdens.

Your clients will then just feel the earnestness & honesty in you & this will set off them to just give them a shot for themselves.

Many partner advertisers commit these errors & are paying the consequences for their activities. To not fall just into similar circumstance they have been in, attempt to do all that to easy Try not to misstep the same way.

Time is the key. Carve out opportunity to dissect your promoting methodology & check assuming you are in the best way. Whenever done appropriately, you will actually really want to boost your member showcasing program & procure higher benefits.

Chapter 7: Simply Finding The Right Product Or Service To Promote

Now that you simply know who your audience is & the niche you really want to be part of, it's time to simply find the right products and/or services to promote to them. There are numerous ways of simply finding the products or services to present to your audience.

• Problems & Solutions

When you have an idea of who your audience is, You can just zero in on sorting out their problems & afterward simply finding solutions to help them. Easy make a rundown of no less than three problems that you really need to address for the audience, in view of the niche you've picked.

Here is an example:
1. Audience: Married working moms of school-aged children who thrive on order
2. Problems: Keeping a family calendar, meal planning, organizing
3. Potential Solutions: Digital calendars, DFY meal plans & shopping lists, organization tips & organization products

When you have a rundown of problems & solutions, go to some known affiliate networks to search for the products you have distinguished as a solid match. A speedy hunt on ClickBank.com - a famous affiliate network where You can just simply find products in any specialty to advertise as well as really Use to advance your own products -uncovers a few products that you should advance, for example, Just get Organized Presently

However, easy Try not to simply begin advancing that now. Easy make a rundown of a few products. Then, do some examination on every item. Easy learn about the maker, just take a gander at the change rate for the item, & contemplate how the maker's qualities & style fit in with the br& voice you really need to show. In the event that you don't simply know somebody who knows them to vouch for their impressive skill, test them out by purchasing the item yourself with the goal that You can just assess the quality of the item & the company for their customer service.

All things considered, as an affiliate advertiser, you are giving your customers to another person to serve. You really want to ensure they will just take great consideration of your customers so your crowd keeps on esteeming your recommendations.

- Different Programs

There are various affiliate networks that rundown opportunities for you to elevate to your crowd. Each has its own eccentricities & issues you'll really need to simply find out about as you join a network. You can just likewise track down affiliate products through direct projects which are not recorded in affiliate networks.

For example, numerous singular distributors simply Utilize technology like aMember.com to set up their program, in which case they won't be recorded on the affiliate platforms. To track down those products, essentially look just into solutions utilizing keywords that you just think will track them down.

For example, in the example above, we looked for a Household Organization on Click Bank. Look for Household Organization on Google to figure out what it shows. The principal bring about our case is a site called Getorganizedgal.com which offers solutions that the crowd would really need & need. Nonetheless, you can't see an affiliate program, yet with more examination she utilizes Workable to convey her courses. Workable has an included affiliate module. You could send her an email making sense of how you like her products furthermore, that your crowd would as well assuming they open an affiliate program for you. One more that shows up is Cozi.com, which is a family coordinator. It incorporates a schedule, shopping records, plans for the day, recipes, & dinner organizer and, surprisingly, a family diary. You can just advance Cozi & bring in cash through their affiliate program if you meet the requirements.

Each network has its upsides & downsides, & there are a lot more than these. You can just simply find enormous arrangements of affiliate networks via searching Google for "affiliate networks," & You can just likewise track down specific networks.

For example, to sell natural products just, you'll track down numerous choices. You can just likewise look just into explicit products you maybe really want to advance, track down a connection to their affiliate program, or email them for information about it.

Some entrepreneurs easy Try not to simply Utilize affiliate networks, yet so many do that you're certain to view as a large number profitable products that You can just advance. Regardless of whether you see one, You can just constantly email the maker to offer your services by showing them your social evidence.

Before you choose an item to advance, you really must look at it regardless of whether the item is profitable. Assuming it's recorded on an affiliate network, You can just see the measurements learned to assist you with deciding how profitable the item is. On the off chance that you are working straightforwardly with an item maker, you maybe have to test your assumptions in the wake of evaluating the item yourself.

Simply finding a profitable item is not exactly that hard assuming that you've picked a decent niche that has a solid audience clamoring for the arrangements they really need to easy make their life better. You must sort out what your niche is, the products your audience necessities, & how you will introduce them to that audience. You can just also easy create your own products for the niche. Let's look at that next.

Another way to easy create a gain as an affiliate marketer is to begin making your own products as well as services to promote to your audience as well. As you work with your audience & gain clients because of the products you promote & the substance you distribute, you maybe acquire understanding just into the audience that gives you the plan to easy make a fresh out of the plastic new item for them. Your item can be free or for a charge, contingent upon how you will simply Utilize it.

One way that You can just include your own products with the blend is by offering a bonus for the purchase of an alternate product for which you are an affiliate. The bonus product offers you the capacity to add them to your rundown, help your income, & maybe show a greater amount of how You can just help the audience with respect to their issues.

Some affiliate systems enable you to add your bonus product right to their funnel on the affiliate platform if the product creator activates that ability for you. In other cases, you may have to just get creative & send the bonus another way. However, there is a lot of technology that will do it automatically for you too.

As an affiliate marketer, You can just easy make your own products that are just for list-building purposes. A genuine model may be an agenda to help your audience pick the right affiliate promoting software or assist them with setting up their first online class. Anything that your audience actually needs & needs that is easy to easy make simply makes a helpful rundown developer.

- Another Income Stream

Furthermore, as an item maker You can just easy make products as a different income stream well beyond your income generation as an affiliate. Perhaps You can just easy make a preferable cleaning association schedule over the one that you've been advancing. Maybe you have composed a course about keeping your home coordinated that you really need to advertise. When you easy make the item, you likewise can enroll affiliates to easy make the sales for you. As an item maker, you'll have to guarantee that you have the right software like aMember.com that assists you with setting up a shopping truck and, surprisingly, an enrollment site that empowers you to disperse your digital products & administrations to your audience. You can just likewise simply Utilize quite a few affiliate networks referenced to list your products What's more, draw in affiliates to help your income.

Simply Finding The Right Affiliates

When you easy make your own products available to be purchased, now is the right time to set up an affiliate program of your own so You can just amplify your range.

Having your own affiliate program resembles having a multitude of salespeople on your site fabricating your business each & every day. Be that as it may, simply finding the right affiliates takes somewhat thought & thought.

Having 1000 affiliates will not help you if they are not good salespeople. If the people who really want to promote your product really Use unscrupulous means to easy make sales, that can also affect you very badly. By focusing on recruiting quality affiliates over a lot of affiliates, You can just simply Avoid most of the problems that can come with affiliates - namely fraud & spam.

Check out any applicants' websites. Do they have an active blog? Does the content fit your audience? Is the website secure? Are they following all the pertinent laws for their couneasy Try & yours regarding spam, privacy, & other issues? Do they appear honest & confident based on the information you simply find on the website?

One way to simply find out about the person behind the website is to do a "Who Is" search. Some of the websites are going to have the information hidden. If that happens, do a little more digging on to ensure that the people behind the site are honest people that you'd really want to deal with in person.

When you go to the site & read the content & information, does it speak to your audience such that they will choose to buy from them? What sort of keywords do they use? Is the content & information direct & above board? Would you just feel safe sending your mother to that site to just get information?

The other thing you will such believe should do when you just get an affiliate is to guarantee that they finish up every one of the right authoritative documents required.
 Regardless of whether you won't convey 1099s since you pay by means of an outsider like PayPal, it is still crucial to just get that data significant on the grounds that it lays out their legitimateness & approves them in a manner that assists you with guarding your customers.

Moreover, have they shown what they can do to be powerful affiliate advertisers? At the point when you are initially beginning as an item merchant, you will be unable to be as well fussy about who becomes affiliates, however in any event guarantee that they are who they say they are, that they are not hoodlums, & that they serve their customers truly & straightforwardly. That's what simply understanding assumes you pick individuals who are new to affiliate marketing, you really want to offer preparation & consolation to them so that they easy make more sales.

Chapter 8: How To Become A Super Affiliate

Throughout the last years, web facilitating has become greater than it used to be. With additional organizations getting just into this business & simply finding the many advantages it can just give them, the interest for web facilitating has never been higher. These appear to be the pattern of today.

This main method a certain something. It is more straightforward now to simply find the right web have for your application. The chance of value web facilitating organizations isolating themselves from the remainder of the business is expected. Assuming this is finished, the amateurish & bumbling ones will endure.

Backing will be the main thought for individuals while picking a web have. It will be clear that customary publicizing will just turn out to be less & less viable. The vast majority would prefer to choose the web have in view of things that they see & hear. Likewise founded on the proposals by the people who have attempted them & have ended up being an effective.

This is an incredible chance for web facilitating partners & affiliates the same. There would many web facilitating & projects to browse that the trouble in simply finding the right one for them is not an issue any longer.

How can one just turn just into an effective subsidiary in the specialty markets utilizing web facilitating?

Looking at the situation objectively, each & every individual who needs a site needs a web facilitating organization to have it for them. At this point, there is actually no driving facilitating industry so the vast majority pick has based from suggestions. As a rule, they just get it from the ones that have previously benefited of a web facilitating administrations.

With the many hosts offering offshoot programs, there is the propensity to simply find the one which you just think will just turn out best for you. Consider the item you will advance. Design them to the site & check whether they are taking care of exactly the same things as you are.

At the point when you have been with one host for a long while & appear to be not to put forth much regardless of all your attempt, leave that one & search for another. There is no utilization in attempting to adhere to one when you would be before off in another. Things will just really need to just get better from that point since you as of now have been in most awful circumstances.

Just give this a shot. On the off chance that you are very blissful & happy with your web have, attempt to check whether they are offering a subsidiary program You can just just take an interest on. Rather than you paying them, why not easy make it the reverse way around; them paying you. The cycle can be basically as simple as putting a little "fueled by" or "facilitated by" connect at the lower part of your page & you are now in a subsidiary business.

Why pick paying for your for your web facilitating as the really need should arise? Attempt to just get compensated by telling individuals you like your web have.

Continuously recollect that while picking a web have, pick the one that is known for its incredible client service. There are likewise many facilitating member programs. Leftover member program is additionally being facilitated. This is the program wherein you just get compensated a rate consistently for a client that you allude. This can permit you to have a consistent type of revenue. With determination, you could simply find success in this field.

There are a ton of specialty markets out there only trusting that the right member will enter to them & easy make that dollars dream materialize. Knowing which one to just get just into is being certain enough of your true capacities & the great outcomes you will get.

Web facilitating is only one offshoot market you could test & easy make some great & nonstop pay. Simply recall that to simply find success on your undertaking additionally implies that time, exertion & persistence is required.

No one has imagined the ideal subsidiary market yet. In any case, certain individuals truly do simply know how to become wildly successful in this sort of market. It is simply knowing your sort of market & making the profit there.

Pose inquiries first before you join an associate program. Do a little research about the decisions of program that you plan to join into. Simply find a few solutions since they will be the concluding mark of what you will accomplish later on.

Will it cost you anything to join? Most associate projects being offered today are totally for nothing. So why settle for those that charge you a few bucks prior to joining.

When do they just give the commission checks? Each program is unique. Some issue their really looks immediately a month, each quarter, & so forth. Select the one that is fit to your installment time decision. Many subsidiary projects are setting a base procured commission sum that a partner should meet or surpass for their checks to be given.

What is the hit per deal proportion? This is the typical number of hits to a pennant or text connect it takes to produce a deal in light of all partner measurements. This component is critical on the grounds that this will let you simply know how much traffic you should produce before You can just procure a commission from the deal.

How are references from an offshoot's site followed & for how long do they stay in the framework? You should be sure on the program to the point of following those individuals you allude from your site. This is the main way that You can just credit for a deal. The timeframe that those individuals stay in the framework is additionally significant. This is on the grounds that a few guests don't buy at first yet maybe really need to just return later to easy make the buy. Simply know whether you will in any case just get kudos for the deal on the off chance that it is done a few months from a specific day.

What are the sorts of partner details accessible? Your decision of associate program ought to be fit for offering point by point details. They ought to be accessible online whenever you choose to look at them.

Continually checking your individual details is critical to simply know the number of impressions, hits & deals that are as of now produced from your site. Impressions are the times the pennant or text interface was seen by a guest of your site. A hit is the one tapping on the flag or text joins.

Does the offshoot program additionally pay for the hits & impressions other than the commissions on deals? It is critical that impressions & hits are likewise paid, as this will add to the profit you just get from the deals commission. This is particularly significant in the event that the program you are in offers low deals to have the option to hit proportion.

Who is the web-based retailer? Figure out whom you are working with to be aware in the event that it is actually a strong organization. Simply know the items they are selling & the typical sum they are accomplishing. The more you realize about the retailer offering you the subsidiary program, the simpler it will be for you to be aware assuming that program is truly for yourself as well as your site.

Is the member a one level or two level program? A solitary level program pays you just for the business you personally have created. A two level program pays you for the business, in addition to it likewise pays you a commission on the on the deals produced by any partner you support in your program. A few two-level projects are in any event, paying little expenses on each new partner you support. More like an enlistment expense.

These are only a portion of the inquiries that required responding to first before you go just into a member program. You ought to be simply know all about the numerous significant angles that your picked program ought to have prior to integrating them just into your site. Attempt to ask your partner program decisions these inquiries. These can assist you with choosing the right program for you site from among the numerous accessible.

There are numerous shocking tales about subsidiary projects & organizations. Individuals have heard them again & again, that some are even careful about going along with one. The accounts they maybe have heard are those

connected with unlawful projects or fraudulent business models. Fundamentally, this sort of market doesn't have genuine, commendable item.

You would rather not be related with these plans. It is clear you really need to be with a program that offers top notch item that you will promptly embrace. The developing number of the people who have joined as of now & are succeeding massively is verification enough that there are solid & quality subsidiary projects out there.

It permits you to work part time . It offers you the chance to construct a liberal leftover pay. Furthermore, it simply makes you a proprietor of a private company. Subsidiary projects have previously made heaps of moguls. They are the living declaration of how difficult work; consistent prospecting, propelling & preparing others pay off.

If at any time you are choosing to go along with one, you should observe that you are getting just into something designed to what you are prepared to do. This will be an affirmation that You can just effectively come out fruitful.

How would you pick a decent partner program to advance? Here are a few hints you maybe really need to investigate prior to picking one:

One of the most mind-blowing approaches to knowing whether that is the sort of program you wish to advance is assuming you are keen on buying the item yourself. Assuming that is the situation, chances are, there are numerous other people who are additionally intrigued by similar program & items.

Each For A Program That Is Of Great.

For example, search for one that is related with numerous specialists in that specific industry. Along these lines, you are guaranteed that of the norm of the program you will join into.

How do you have any idea about this? Do some underlying examination. If conceivable, simply find a portion of the individuals & clients to just give you tribute on the validity of the program.

This will guarantee you that there will be more & consistent requests for your references. Easy make requests. There are gatherings & conversations You can just just take part in to just get great & dependable criticisms.

program with a pay plan that pays out a leftover pay & a payout of 40% or more would be an extraordinary decision.

Some subsidiary projects forces pre-requirements before you just get your payments. Simply be certain that you are equipped for accomplishing their necessities.

The partner program that gives consistent assistance & moves up to its items tend to hold its individuals. These things can guarantee the development of your organizations.

Simply know about the things that individuals are disturbed about in a program.

Like with the ones referenced above, You can just do your checking at conversation discussions. Assuming you simply know somebody in that equivalent program, there is ho hurt inquiring as to whether there are numerous drawbacks included.

Have a careful & serious information about the subsidiary program & organization you will advance on.

Knowing the sort of program you are simply finding yourself mixed up with will really Use you to expect & forestall any future issues you maybe experience.

Easy allow us to investigate how PPC Web indexes work.

These motors easy make postings & rate them in light of a bid sum the site proprietor will pay for each click from that web search tool. Sponsors bid against one another to just get higher positioning for a particular watchword or expression.

The most elevated bidder for a specific catchphrase or expression will then, at that point, have the site positioned as number 1 in the PPC Web crawlers followed continuously & third most noteworthy bidder, up to the last number that have put a bid on a similar watchword or expression. Your advertisements then, at that point, will show up conspicuously on the outcomes pages in view of the dollar sum bid you will consent to pay per click.

How would you bring in cash by utilizing PPC just into your associate showcasing business?

Most offshoot programs possibly pay when a deal is made or a lead conveyed after a guest has click through your site. Your income won't generally be equivalent to they will be subject to the site content & the traffic market.

The motivation behind why you ought to integrate PPC just into your subsidiary showcasing program is that profit are more straightforward to easy make than in some other sort of member program not utilizing PPC. Along these lines, you will easy create gain based from the clickthroughs that your guest will easy make on the sponsor's site. Dissimilar to certain projects, you are not paid per deal or activity.

PPC can be extremely creative of your site. With PPC Web indexes integrated just into your

member program, you will actually really want to benefit from the guest's who are not intrigued by your items or administrations. Similar ones who leave your site & never returns.

You won't just just get commissions not just from the individuals who are simply looking through the web & tracking down the items & administrations that they needed however you will actually really want to fabricate your webpage's acknowledgment as a significant asset. The guests who have found what they required from you site are probably going to just return & audit what you are offering all the more intently. Then, at that point, they will ultimately just return to scan the web for different items.

This sort of associate program is likewise a simple way for you to produce a few additional extra incomes. For instance, when a guest on your site does a hunt in the PPC Web search tool & clicks on the publicist awaited postings, the promoters' record will then be deducted due to that click. With
this, you will be repaid 30% to 80% of the publicists' offered sum.

PPC is not just a wellspring of producing simple benefits; it can likewise assist you with advancing your own site. A large portion of the projects permit the commissions really got to be spent for publicizing with them in a split second & with no base procuring necessity. This is one of the more successful ways of trading your crude guests for designated surfers who has more inclinations to buy your items & administrations.

What will occur on the off chance that you when you coordinate PPC just into your associate program?

PPC typically have prepared to-simply Utilize member devices that can be effectively coordinated just into your site. The most widely recognized devices are search boxes, standards, text connections & a few 404-misjust take pages. Most web crawlers really Use custom arrangements & can just give you a white-mark partner program. This empowers you, utilizing a couple of lines of code, to incorporate remotely-facilitated co-marked web crawler just into your site.

The key advantages? More cash produced as well as some additional cash as an afterthought. Besides a lifetime commissions whenever you have alluded some website admin companions to the motor.

Consider it. Where maybe you at any point just get this multitude of advantages while previously simply creating some pay for your site? Knowing a portion of the more helpful devices You can just really Use for your partner program is definitely not an exercise in futility. They are somewhat a method for procuring inside a procuring.

Best simply find out about how You can just simply Utilize PPC web search tools just into your offshoot program than pass up an extraordinary chance to procure more benefits.

Chapter 9: Affiliate Marketing: What To Simply Avoid

As with any other business that involves making money, affiliate marketing is vulnerable to various forms of fraud, including cookie-stuffing & dropping. There are some other approaches you should bypass, including:

Some affiliates may deceive buyers by offering them products they don't really need or failing to tell the whole story about an item. If you easy make bold statements, you maybe just get more traffic, but it would be unethical & could violate the law.

Chapter 10: Track Your Affiliate Marketing Success

As with everything else, you can't tell if your marketing efforts are working unless you've really got some metric for measuring them.

You can just start by checking your affiliate program's dashboard to see how much you made. But You can just also really Use other tools to track stats for individual channels. For example, if you're an affiliate simply Using Google Ad Sense, You can just check your earnings from the Google Ads Dashboard.

These metrics will assist you to understand how often people click on links & how often they purchase from your site. Pay attention to which types of content are most effective at driving sales & easy create more of that kind of content.

Pose inquiries first before you join an associate program. Do a little research about the decisions of program that you expect to join into. Simply find a few solutions since they will be the concluding mark of what you will accomplish later on.

Will it cost you anything to join? Most associate projects being offered today are totally for nothing. So why settle for those that charge you a few bucks prior to joining.

When do they just give the commission checks? Each program is unique. Some issue their really takes a look immediately a month, each quarter, & so forth. Select the one that is fit to your installment time decision. Many partner programs are setting a base procured commission sum that a member should meet or surpass for their checks to be given.

What is the hit per deal proportion? This is the typical number of hits to a flag or text connect it takes to easy create a deal in light of all member measurements. This component is critical on the grounds that this will let you simply know how much traffic you should produce before You can just procure a commission from the deal.

How are references from a partner's site followed & for how long do they stay in the framework? You should be certain on the program to the point of following those individuals you allude from your site. This is the main way that You can just credit for a deal. The timeframe that those individuals stay in the framework is likewise significant. This is on the grounds that a few guests don't buy at first however maybe really need to just return later to easy make the buy.

Simply know whether you will in any case just get kudos for the deal in the event that it is done a few months from a specific day.

What are the sorts of partner details accessible? Your decision of associate program ought to be equipped for offering itemized details. They ought to be accessible online whenever you choose to look at them. Continually checking your individual details is essential to simply know the number of impressions, hits & deals that are now created from your site.

Impressions are the times the standard or text connect was seen by a guest of your site. A hit is the one tapping on the pennant or text joins.

Does the partner program additionally pay for the hits & impressions other than the commissions on deals? It is critical that impressions & hits are likewise paid, as this will add to the profit you just get from the deals commission. This is particularly significant assuming the program you are in offers low deals to have the option to hit proportion.

Who is the web-based retailer? Figure out whom you are working with to be aware in the event that it is actually a strong organization. Simply know the items they are selling & the typical sum they are accomplishing. The more you realize about the retailer offering you the member program, the simpler it will be for you to be aware assuming that program is truly for yourself as well as your site.

Is the subsidiary a one level or two level program? A solitary level program pays you just for the business you personally have created. A two level program pays you for the business, in addition to it likewise pays you a commission on the on the deals produced by any offshoot you support in your program. A few two-level projects are in any event, paying little charges on each new partner you support. More like an enrollment charge.

Ultimately, what is how much commission paid? 5% - 20% is the commission paid by most projects. .01% - .05% is the sum paid for each hit. Assuming that you simply find a program that likewise pays for impressions, the sum paid is not a lot of in any way. As You can just see from the figures, you will currently comprehend the reason why the typical deals sum & hit to deal proportion is significant.

These are only a portion of the inquiries that required responding to first before you go just into a subsidiary program. You ought to be simply know about the numerous significant perspectives that your picked program ought to have prior to integrating them just into your site. Attempt to ask your member program decisions these inquiries. These can assist you with choosing the right program for you site from among the numerous accessible.

This is The way To Simply Avoid The 3 Most Common Affiliate Mistakes

Member advertising is one of the best & strong approaches to bringing in some cash on the web. This program allows everyone an opportunity to easy create a gain through the Internet. Since these partner promoting programs are not difficult to join, carry out & pays a commission consistently, more an additional group are currently willing around here.

Notwithstanding, similar to all organizations, there are bunches of entanglements in the member promoting business. Committing probably the most well-known mix-ups will cost the advertisers an enormous piece taken from the benefit they are making regular. To that end staying away from them than be remorseful in the end is better.

Choosing Some Unacceptable Partner Program.

Many individuals really need to procure from offshoot advertising as quick as could really be expected.

In their hurry to be crucial for one, they will generally pick a fad item. This is the sort of items that they such believe is "hot". They pick the item that is popular without really considering if

The item requests to them. This is definitely not an extremely savvy move clearly.

Rather than getting on board with that fleeting trend, attempt top pick an item in which you are really keen on. For any undertaking to succeed, you ought to set aside some margin to plan & sort out your activities.

Pick an item that requests to you. Then in all actuality do an examination about that item to check whether they are popular. Advancing an item you are

more enthusiastic about is simpler than advancing one for the profit as it were.

Since partner programs are exceptionally simple to go along with, you may be enticed to join products of associate projects to attempt to amplify the income you will get. Other than you maybe imagine that everything is all good & nothing to lose by being essential for some member programs.

Valid, that is an incredible method for having various types of revenue. Notwithstanding, joining different projects & endeavoring to advance them all simultaneously will keep you from focusing on every single one of them.

The outcome? The greatest capability of your subsidiary program is not understood & the pay produced won't precisely be basically as immense as you were suspecting at first it would. The most effective way to obtain incredible outcome is by joining only one program that pays a 40% commission in any event.

Then just give it your maximum effort by advancing your items excitedly. When you see that it is simply creating a sensible gain, then perhaps You can just now join another member program.

The procedure is to do it gradually. There is actually compelling reason really need to race just into things, particularly with member showcasing. With the status quo going, what's in store is looking genuinely brilliant & it appears offshoot showcasing will remain for quite a while as well.

Chapter 11: Affiliate Most Tricks Marketing?

Affiliate marketing is a marketing model designed so that individuals can help companies sell more of their products & services both online & offline.

As an affiliate marketer you will work within a referral based system that allows you to earn a cut of the money that companies easy make from sales made to people that you refer.

For example: There are two acquaintances, let's call them Johanna & Ruth

Johanna is the owner of an crucial retail store. Every year she spends millions of dollars in marketing & advertising in order to attract new customers.

One days she comes out with a plan.

Rather than continue to spend more money on advertising, she decides to just give her friend Ruth a special number so that she can just give to people who may be interested in shopping at Johanna's store. Ruth begins handing out the numbers to different people & these people go & shop at Johanna's store.

Johanna knows when Ruth sends a new customer, because the customers will have Ruth's special number with them. Thus every time a customer with Ruth's number shops from Johanna's store, Johanna will share a small percentage of that sale with Ruth as an incentive.

In a nutshell, this is exactly how affiliate marketing works.

How Much Can You Easy make With Affiliate Marketing?

The amount of money that You can just earn with affiliate marketing will depend on the product that you choose to promote. Often times, this amount can be up to 100% of the total price of the product.

All & all, if I was to summarize affiliate marketing in five basic points, they would be:
You partner with a company to help them promote a product or service.

You market & send traffic to these products simply Using your own resources.

Some of those people purchase the product based on your recommendation.

You just get paid a commission for those purchases.

Affiliate marketing is one of the best & easiest ways for anyone to easy make money online. It is a billion dollar a year industry with a very low barrier of entry. You do not really need any special degrees or high technical knowledge to easy make it work, the door is pretty much open to anyone willing to step inside.

You can just start with no investment

Affiliate marketing does not require a big initial investment. If you are strapped on cash, there are plenty of free strategies that You can just really Use in order to simply find people on the internet who are interested in buying whatever you promote.

You can just work from anywhere in the world

You can just work from anywhere in the world, all you really need is a computer & an internet connection.

Affiliate marketing is for people willing to easy create a new source of income simply Using the internet. Whether you are looking to easy make an extra $100 a month, $550 per month, or even $1,500,000 a month, affiliate marketing can be a way to just get there.

When done right, affiliate marketing is an excellent way to easy make really good money online.

If you are an overachiever & dedicate yourself enough to master the affiliate marketing game, You can just earn incredible amounts of money right from the comfort of your home or anywhere in the world, as long as you have a computer & an internet connection at hand.

The right approach to affiliate marketing

Affiliate marketing is beautiful when done in a way that adds value to people. In other words, do not just get just into affiliate marketing if you plan to spam people with offers from products that you simply know won't help them. If you do it this way, other than not making many sales, You can just end up pissing off a lot of people.

As an affiliate marketer your job is to identify a really need in the market, simply find a solution that satisfies that really need & put that solution in front of the people who really need it. It's simple! I have had people thank me before for selling them an affiliate product and, in my opinion, that is the way that it should be.

Chapter 12: How To Just Get Started With Affiliate Marketing

The first thing that you really need to do in order to just get started with affiliate marketing is to determine the niche (product category) that you will like to promote.

It is crucial that you do this step right & just take your time to do good research on the product & your chosen audience.

Good market research will help you to determine whether your product is worth promoting or if you will be better off promoting something else.

Some of the best niches to just get just into this year are:

Evergreen niches- Evergreen niches are product categories that can be sold all year round to a large demographic.

For example, people from all over the world really want to lose weight all the time, therefore this could be a really good niche to just get into. Now do keep in mind that this niche may already be saturated with competition & could be a bit difficult for a complete as a newbie to just get into, unless you already have a following of raving fans on the internet or an amazing marketing strategy that will put you above the competition. Other evergreen niches are, hair loss, acne, dog training, dating, finance, self-help, etc.

Seasonal niches- seasonal niches are product categories that can only be sold within a certain period of time or to a certain demographic. For example, if you

Viral products- These are products that gain overwhelming amounts of popularity within a very short period of time. These viral trends can last for as little as a month, to as long as a year. A good example of a viral product is the famous fidjust get spinner. These little toys gained wide popularity within kids & even some adults. Catching a viral product in & promoting it during its infancy, can like winning the internet lottery.

Tip- One quick way to simply find out if you have a marketable product is to look for some competition. If other marketers are already promoting a product or products similar to yours, it could mean that there is money to be made within your niche.

The method that you choose to really Use will have a direct effect on the amount of time that it will just take you to see results. See it this way, if you lived & L.A but wanted to just get to New York, there will be more than one way to do it.

If you really want to just get there fast, You can just buy a plane ticket, which can cost you money, but You can just easy make it there in a few hours.

If you wanted to just get there & didn't mind how long & how much effort it took you, You can just just take the journey by foot, which will save you money, but it can be months before you arrive at your destination.

My point is that regardless of the method you choose to adopt, you will have to sacrifice something one way or another.

You can just either invest a few dollars to buy tools that can easy make your job a lot easier & simply achieve results faster, or You can just "save" a few dollars, do everything by hand, sacrifice valuable time & effort, to hopefully see results after months, or even years.

Nevertheless, I do not really want to discard either one of these methods because people have made money simply Using both & you will have to decide on the one that adapts best to your goals or current financial circumstances.

In order to help you easy make a more informed decision, here is a more in depth explanation for each.

Free methods can just take a bit more work & obtaining results can be slower than if you really Use paid methods, but it is indeed still very possible to easy create a lucrative affiliate marketing business simply Using free resources.

The only real advantage about getting started with affiliate marketing for free is that it can save you a few bucks, other than that I can't just think of anything else that could be beneficial in only simply Using this strategy.

In order to easy make a free method work, you will have to do it right. As mentioned, getting started for free will require some patience, as well as a good strategy. Here is a free strategy that You can just really Use in order to just get started with your affiliate marketing business today:

Easy create accounts on free social media platforms like Facebook, YouTube, Twitter & Instagram.

Join multiple Facebook groups related to your niche.

Just give as much value as possible to those groups. Do not sell anything at first, simply just take time to answer people's questions, like other people's posts, be friendly & easy create new connections.

Once you have gained people's trust, begin to share links to your own social media accounts & encourage people to follow you.

Continue adding value, both within your page & Facebook groups.

After you have created a good following on your own pages, You can just start promoting affiliate products or services.

Start making some money.

You can just combine multiple free methods at once. For example, You can just easy create a YouTube channel or a free blog simply Using platforms like wix or weebly & upload great content related to your niche, then post the links to this content on the Facebook groups.

YouTube is not only a great way to just get free traffic, but also to easy build an audience. In fact, YouTube is now considered the second largest search engine on the internet today! You can just really Use Facebook groups in your niche to simply find out what topics people are most interested in & easy create blog posts or videos within these interests. This could be a great way to drive larger amounts of traffic to your content & increase the possibility of making sales

The Paid Method

This is the method that I really Use & has given me the best results, therefore I highly encourage anyone serious about getting just into affiliate marketing to invest the time just into mastering this approach instead.

Investing some money just into your affiliate marketing business will enable you to grow your business at a much faster pace. A marketing budjust get will enable you to test products a lot faster rather than doing it in an organic way.

For example, it can just take you many months to just get things rolling with a blog or growing a YouTube channel. You will have to spend many hours simply creating content & marketing this content on your own. You will more than likely have to visit countless forums or Facebook pages, & tirelessly share a link to your website or YouTube video with anyone you interact with. Then all you have left is hope that people will click on your link & visit your website & pray that these visits can l& you an affiliate sale. Rather, by just bucks a month, you will be able to just get access to tools that will easy make your life 10x easier, & easy allow you to collect data that could help you to reach your goals a lot faster. The amount of money that you invest just into getting started with paid affiliate marketing will solely depend on you, & most of this money should be used on purchasing traffic to test offers.

If your marketing approach is to grow an audience organically, You can just just get started with as little as $12 a month for hosting & a domain then really Use the free strategy above to drive free traffic to your website & offers. Keep in mind that this can still just take some time & effort to easy make it work. In order to just get started with the paid method, you will really need a few tools. These tools are essential because they easy allow you to systemize the entire process, & once you have it figured out, to pretty much easy make money on auto-pilot. Here are the tools you will really need access to in order to do paid affiliate marketing the right way. Offer - This is the product that will be promoted to earn a commission every time you generate a sale. These could be physical or digital products & services. Typically, You can just just get a product to promote for free from one of the affiliate platforms mentioned below. Website or op-in page (Landing Page)- As mentioned earlier, the website can be a blog where you write articles about your chosen niche & recommend products within the content of your articles for your readers to purchase or a capture page. A capture page, also referred as lander, landing page, or squeeze page, is a page specifically designed to capture someone's information such as their name, email or phone number. Capturing potential customers information is extremely important, & a part that you can't leave out of your marketing strategy, I'll explain in a further section why. Traffic - These are people (visitors) that could be interested in your product. You can just just get traffic by purchasing it from different platforms or for free by growing a sizable following of people interested in your content. Click tracker- This is software that allows you to track the number of people that click on your links. For example, with this tool you will be able to simply know how Lot's of people clicked on your link but never purchased, allowing you to optimize (change wording, color, or structure) of your landing page or website. This tool is essential in order to scale your business to thousands of dollars a day as it will help you to identify which offer attracts more visitors than others. Auto responder- the auto responder is a software that will easy allow you to send automatic emails to the people who sign up to your email list through your landing page. According to the way you set it, the software will automatically send pre-determined emails by date, purchase type, or action type, to people who have subscribed to your email list. We will discuss more about the importance of simply creating an email list in the sections below. Now that you simply know briefly what you will need, let's go more in depth on how these tools interconnect & how to successfully really Use them to easy create a profitable affiliate marketing business.

The type of product that you decide to promote can have a direct impact on the amount of money that you make. With affiliate marketing, you must understand that some products are always in more dem& than others. For example, there is a higher dem& for weight loss products than for weight gain products. So, knowing this, you should simply know that you will be more likely to generate sales by promoting products in the weight loss niche than by promoting products for people who are trying to gain weight. Your job as an affiliate marketer is to simply find products in high demand, even better when these products solve people's problems. The products that you promote as an affiliate can be both physical or digital. Lets dive a bit deeper just into each one of them. But right here, we are going to be focusing solely on the digital products, so let's just get right just into it.

How to promote digital products

In order to promote digital products you will have to join an affiliate network. An affiliate network is a third party company that hosts multiple digital and, on some occasions, physical products for affiliates to promote. They are basically the middle man between the product creator & you.

One reason why promoting products through affiliate networks is crucial is because they easy make sure that you just get the right compensation for the sales that you generate. Let's be honest, the internet can be shady. If you are not careful with who you work with, You can just spend countless hours of your time working on promoting a product & generating sales for a product creator only for them to deny your commissions payout. Affiliate networks easy make sure that product creators are who they say that they are, & that publishers just get the compensation that we deserve for helping these product creators to generate sales. Affiliate networks also easy make sure that guidelines are followed, they often also test products before they easy allow affiliates to promote them. In a way, they help us affiliates to be safer when doing business with other people on the internet.

A lot of these networks will also help you with training & guidance because it is in their best interest that you easy create as many sales as possible. Today, there are thousands of affiliate networks eager to work with anyone willing to promote their products, like on anything else, it is crucial to do your research & simply find out which affiliate network best fits your affiliate marketing goals.

How to become a digital affiliate

Nowadays, many companies & websites employ affiliate marketers to promote their goods & services but the best part is that most companies require nothing or small amount of money to just get started with their products so this is a very useful info if you have small or no money to start affiliate marketing

These are just small companies that require free registration but I am sure that if you extend your research, you'll simply find many other companies willing to collect nothing from you

Website Or Landing Page

Today, not having a website should no longer be an excuse. Content delivery networks like WordPress have made it extremely easy for anyone to easy create beautiful & professional looking websites in a matter of minutes, even without having to spend hundreds of hours sitting in front of a computer learning HTML, CSS & JavaScript.

A website plays a very crucial role in affiliate marketing, more so when you incorporate it just into your marketing strategy.

Having your own website is essential because it will help you easy build trust with potential customers. It will easy make you more professional in your potential customers eyes.

If you such believe that simply creating a website could be that tedious task that can keep you from simply achieving any type of success with affiliate marketing, do not worry, our free mini course will show you how to easy make a professional website fast in just a few hours!

A website can be used in a few different ways, but the way that you really Use to integrate it to your marketing plan will ultimately depend on the strategy that you decide to follow.

Growing An Email List The Right Way

A customer's email list, when used correctly, is used to interact, help, & generate trust with your subscribers. An email list is NOT another way to spam subscribers with unsolicited offers daily or sell them on crappy products with the sole purpose to just take their money. Once you grow your list to thousand it will become a great asset to your business because you will no longer have to rely on paid traffic to reach potential customers.

Here is how an email list works
 Let's say that you promote a product on the weight loss niche. In order to just get people just into your list, you must first just target them with a free offer. This could be something like a free report on "the top 10 foods that easy make you gain weight", or "the 10 foods

you should simply Avoid if you really want to lose weight fast", pretty much anything that these people will be interested in. Your free offer should simply Provide good information & add value to their lives, & the image used should portray something worth giving away an email address for.

Once you have your free offer ready, you will then send traffic to a landing page created with the sole purpose to encourage visitors to exchange their best email address for the free report, just like the one above. Your goal is to just get as Lot's of people to subscribe to your list as you possibly can, because once they do, You can just continue to reach out to them without having to purchase traffic from expensive traffic sources.

Again, simply creating an email list should not only be about the money, you should also be dedicated to truly help these people with their problems & become their go-to person for questions & advice. If you do this right, these people will not just think twice about investing in the products & services that you recommend & you will not only easy make really good commission, but some of them will also invite their friends & family members to join your list, helping you to grow it without spending money on buying traffic.

Traffic

You can just have the best product in the world but if no one knows that it exists, you will not easy make any sales. Traffic, & most importantly, the quality of traffic that you just get to your offers will have a direct effect on the amount of sales that you generate. There are thousands of ways that You can just just get traffic to your offers, You can just do it simply Using free methods & paid methods.

Free traffic

As we discussed earlier, You can just harness the power of platforms like Facebook & YouTube to easy create large followings & just get free traffic to your offers.

Paid traffic

There are many ways to purchase traffic, but keep in mind that driving traffic to your offers alone will not be sufficient to money online with affiliate marketing. In order to easy make paid traffic work, you will really need to simply know your offer & the type of people who will be more inclined to buy it.

Before you invest money on paid traffic, just take some time with pen & paper on h& & write down the top 10 characteristics of the perfect customer for your product. What does your customer look like? What is your customer's gender? How old is he/she? What are their hobbies? What do they struggle with the most that your product will help them fix or improve? Where do they work? Where do they eat out? How much do they easy make a year? Are they timid, shy, lonely, etc. Easy create the perfect avatar of your potential buyer & proceed from there. Simply creating a potential customer avatar will help you to position your offer from the most effective angle. An angle in affiliate marketing is a distinctive approach that your potential customer will be able to identify with the most. Once you have created your perfect avatar & decided on the angle, it's time to purchase traffic.

Knowing how to purchase & drive quality traffic to your offers is an essential skill in making money online. Once you master this, you will not only be able to drive traffic to your offers, but will also be able to really Use it for other marketing purposes, such as driving traffic to your own business or charging businesses in your local area for your paid advertising services. From there, technically, the possibilities to easy make money become endless.

Learning to effectively drive paid traffic is extremely important. If you do not just take the time to easy learn paid traffic, You can just spend thousands of dollars purchasing it & never easy make a cent back. I highly recommend you to easy learn as much as You can just on how to purchase & drive traffic to your offers. Do not be afraid to invest money in books, courses, seminars & anything else that will help you master it, because once you do, you will be literally able to print money online. Below I'll explain briefly how paid traffic works & where to just get it from.

Chapter 13: How To Become A Super Affiliate In Niche Markets

Now that affiliate marketing is popular, Lot's of people are becoming self-represented in this line of work. But as the competition increases, you maybe really need some strategies to set yourself apart from the other affiliate marketers.

The main cause is that you & many of your rivals are advertising the same application in the same area or even on the same websites.

Here is some advice that you maybe just take just into account if you really want to stay in business & have a chance to outsmart & outshine your rivals.

The first step is for you to have a website of your own.

If you really want to pursue a career in affiliate marketing, having your website is necessary.

Second, prospective clients visit websites mostly to conduct product searches & occasionally easy make purchases. For the same reason, you may simply direct users to the affiliate page on your website rather than having them remember a specific URL that you may be employing.

Having your ad is another thing to keep in mind.

Affiliate marketers frequently publish the same advertisement from an advertiser twice or three times. If so, send an email to the administrator of your affiliate program requesting that they easy create your advertising. By doing this, people may not develop an immunity to advertisements, as seeing the same advertising repeatedly may force some of your potential clients to simply ignore them. In addition, your main goal is to entice or motivate people to click on, read, & be interested in your adverts & website.

Step three is to have some of your products that are solely sold on your website.

Once your website is up & running, it is crucial to offer certain goods or services that your clients cannot discover on the websites of other affiliates. The greatest method to ensure that visitors to your website keep coming back is to simply Provide them with something they can't just get elsewhere. The next step is to select a market area as an affiliate marketer where You can just potentially play a leadership or at the very least a strong challenger role.

Building a solid relationship with customers who have previously purchased your goods is the fourth phase.

Now, it is best to attempt & purchase the goods on your own if you as the marketer really want to properly address the question of your potential clients. With this specific idea, You can just more effectively market the thing you're trying to sell. Your positive experience with the goods can pique the curiosity of potential customers & convince them to purchase the item. Depending on your own experience, you maybe also be able to offer assistance, or you maybe confidently demonstrate how to simply Utilize the product you're attempting to sell. Being truthful about the product you're trying to sell is implied by this principle. Stop advertising the program you were endorsing & let your readers simply know if you easy learn that it is a hoax. You can just establish credibility with your lists by doing this. We all easy make mistakes, & by acknowledging your own, you'll increase your reader's trust in you.

Finally, simply Avoid trying to sell everything you come across.

It is simple to just get overwhelmed when simply Using services like click bank & trying to promote everything there. That's not a wise move. It is preferable to concentrate on one market & sell them items they would want. The term for this is specialized marketing.

Additionally, easy make an effort to advertise a product that meets the criteria determined by customer satisfaction indicators rather than indicators of self-gratification. The customer, not the business or the affiliate marketer, chooses what to purchase. The business merely creates products to meet the demands & preferences of the market group they have chosen.

Chapter 14: Affiliate Marketing Business With Little Start-Up Fund

I just think it is clear to you that you may start affiliate marketing without any money. We are fortunate to be living in a time when there are several free social media sites with sizable, ready-made specialized audiences. Spend time simply creating your message & interacting with your audience on the channels you have selected. It does really need perseverance, energy, & work, but if You can just persevere, you will eventually be rewarded. When you do begin earning commissions, I strongly advise spending money on a website & a mentor to help you advance. In order to maintain your business growth over time, investing in it is crucial.

Although it is possible to launch an internet business at no cost, it takes work to easy make it profitable. Your affiliate marketing business must be established, then you must continue to grow it while interacting with customers & providing them with value.

How Should A Website For Affiliate Marketing Be Set Up?

Starting an affiliate marketing business doesn't really need having a flashy, pricey website. It is more than sufficient to increase conversions if the website has a polished appearance, is simple to use, & has engaging content & persuasive sales text. Several websites, like carrd.co, wix, & others, are available for really Use without charge.

How To Start Your Affiliate Marketing Business Without A Website

Despite the fact that landing pages or your own website are what most affiliate marketers use, you may begin affiliate marketing without either. To be present online & produce leads, you do not necessarily really need to manage your own website. These are three other strategies for conducting affiliate marketing without a website:

Social media: You can just share affiliate product links if you have a sizable social media following or are a prominent figure in online forums & groups.

YouTube: Video is one of the most powerful marketing tools, & many affiliate marketers simply Utilize it to advertise their products & increase conversion rates on YouTube. If you easy make videos, you maybe choose to easy create an active YouTube channel than a standard website.

Email marketing: You may send affiliate offers via email if you have an email list. For affiliates, email may be a potent performance marketing tool.

Which Products Are The Best For Affiliate Marketing?

For affiliate marketing products, there are countless alternatives. Easy Try picking a product that interests you or about which you are at least slightly aware, especially if you really want to become a relevant or active affiliate marketer. Easy make sure you pick a specialized market with strong dem& & monetization possibilities for its goods & services. Naturally, this will also easy make these niches extremely competitive, but you really need to be sure that there is a market for the goods you're pushing.

What Are Some Ways To Produce Content For Affiliate Marketing?

Content is your primary tool for profit as an affiliate marketer. The hook that draws the just target audience in & encourages them to engage on your affiliate links is your content, & that's what will bring in the cash.

In affiliate marketing, you may employ a wide range of content. Blogs are one of the most popular. The process of starting a blog is quite straightforward, & if you are knowledgeable with the subject matter or industry, You can just easily share your knowledge & excitement, which results in fascinating material.

Additionally, you may produce reviews, ebooks, videos, landing sites, & more.

You can just always outsource content creation if you're not a natural writer or do not have the time to devote to it yourself. There are a ton of article writing businesses out there that offer good material for fair costs.

Should I Pursue Affiliate Marketing?

Only You can just truly determine whether affiliate marketing is a suitable fit for your personality & skill set. In the end, it's up to you. As an affiliate, you may easy make money, sometimes a lot of it, but you really need to be sure that you're doing it from the heart & that the goods & services you're promoting are useful to & appropriate for your just target market. Here are a few things to just think about before choosing:

- Starting up doesn't require a significant investment.
- You must be inventive & eager to continually picking up new web. Tools & techniques.
- You really need to have patience. It takes time & work to establish a profitable affiliate marketing business.
- Your online actions really need to be optimized, fine-tuned, & continually monitored for outcomes
- If you genuinely care about & such believe in the services or deals you are marketing, you will succeed.
- You must possess the capacity to establish a reliable, approachable web presence. You'll just get traffic because of this.

Do You Really need To Leave Your Job To Work In Affiliate Marketing?

It maybe just take time & perseverance to really Use affiliate marketing to easy make a full-time living. It's often not advised to leave your regular work until you are generating enough funds to cover what you are now making. If you do decide to stop your job & have some savings to fall back on, you will discover that you'll have more time to concentrate on your business, which may easy allow you to grow & earn more quickly. However, if you do not have any savings, the good news is that You can just still start an affiliate marketing business while working a full-time job. Even while your workday may be short on time, if you easy make the most of it, you may start a new affiliate business with no risk & have the money to pay for a course that will help you advance more quickly.

Simply Utilize the downtime you have between other obligations to work on up to three primary tasks for your affiliate marketing business. You'll start seeing results if you start making it a habit to do three tasks each day for your affiliate company & concentrate on improving every day.

Be patient with yourself while you easy learn the fundamentals, & do not be hard on yourself if you easy make mistakes or just get things wrong. Any new business requires learning, & setbacks may teach you a lot if you easy allow them. You will start earning commissions if you stay motivated, keep moving forward, & continue to simply Provide value in your chosen affiliate marketing industry. As a result, you will eventually be able to just quit your day job & live a life of independence while earning a full-time living through affiliate marketing.

Chapter 15: How To Super Sell Simply Using Email

Selling by email is different than selling on a sales page. Sales letters have to work under the impression that they have just one shot to easy make a sale & have to hammer in all the benefits & go for an instant close. Email on the other h& has the benefit of a relationship & ongoing contact.

Aim to first easy build trust & reader loyalty. This is what will just get your emails opened time after time. Once your emails are getting opened & you have your reader's trust, then You can just safely easy make sale after sale without alienating your list.

If you sell too much without first building trust, readers are more likely to tune out than buy. So how do you easy build this trust?

Simply Provide first class, unique, original content that directly benefits the reader. Every time they read an email from you or buy a product from you, they should be better off. Do this consistently & readers will start to such believe in you & your products.

Once of these is the Problem > Problem > Problem > Solution formula. Simply put, you send a series of emails about just the problem without offering a solution (yet). You can just simply Provide a lot of value by just explaining the problem. Then you finally offer an innovative & powerful solution.

If you have strong readership, by the time readers just get your "solution" email they'll be dying to just get their hands on the product. Easy build up the problem while providing value, then simply Provide the solution when they're already ready to buy.

Another effective way of generating sales is to really Use teleseminars. Really Use a teleseminar to demonstrate knowledge in a particular arena, & then really Use emails to follow up & close the sale. Finally, every once in a while offer a sale. Perhaps it's your birthday sale, or a favorite day of the year sale; whatever the reason is, just a few times a year offer a sale of 15% to 30% off. You'll easy make much more than the amount you lose on discounts.

Conclusion

There you have it! If you have made it this far, you now simply know enough to start your very own affiliate marketing business. After reading this guide, you should no longer have an excuse as to why You can just never easy make any money online. Just take this information to heart, read this guide more than once if really need to, & implement the information to start right away. Do not let all this learning simply lead to knowledge, let it lead to action, that is the only way that you will simply achieve your goals.

www.ingramcontent.com/pod-product-compliance
Lightning Source LLC
Chambersburg PA
CBHW071629080526
44588CB00010B/1334